WHAT'S IN IT FOR ME?

Table Of Contents

ADDITIONAL MOMENTUM ENHANCEMENT OPTIONS

On-Line Interactive eCourse at www.JeffreyMagee.com

Weekly eZine Subscription for the **Leadership Moment©** at www.JeffreyMagee.com

eBook Delivery Systems at www.KeysToMySuccess.com , www.WIIFM.org and www.WIIFM.us, email to WIIFM@cox.net

Preface
Tuning in to the Explosive
Frequency of WIIFM.US

Tuning in to the explosive frequency of "What's in it for me" and "What's in it for us" is all about business and your career advancement, for both today and tomorrow.

What the heck do you want out of life? What the heck do you want to be? Don't know? Don't worry! But remember, "Yesterday is gone forever; tomorrow is yet to be...!" It's a brand new world every morning, and there are no guarantees! You must get up, get out, and take full advantage of the explosive powers you possess, all the while asking yourself, "What's in it for me?"

However you decide What's in it for me *in your career, just ensure you continually use the two explosive mental points of reference below as benchmarks in all that you do and all that you convey to others, and you will never be without a paycheck:*

1. How do I generate revenue in what I do?
2. How do I save revenue in what I do?

Consider just how easy it is to be successful today. Think of basic gravity and the lessons learned here and extrapolated for your success endeavors. If you stand up, lean forward. What are the most obvious two outcomes of that act? One, you will fall forward and, thus, down. Second, you will begin to fall forward, but you will make a "choice" in a very calculated manner to move forward!

The difference between success and lack thereof is all in the subtraction of four letters. Yes, four letters.

If you take the word "success" - to attain, to move forward, to aspire, to accomplish, to be measured above others, to ascend onward and upward - and subtract the last four letters of the word, you phonetically arrive at a second, more powerful word.

A "What's in it for me" mentality is neither right nor wrong. It is simply one's mentality! It's not being selfish!

You must look out for yourself in order to take care of friends, family, a business, etc...

And, yes, now you have arrived. The difference between these two destinations is that successful individuals have identified those things at which they excel and have applied themselves there. They also have identified those things at which they are not successful, and they don't pursue them!

WOW! There is a powerful thought!

In tuning in to the explosive frequency of What's in it for me and What's in it for us, one can recognize 52 powerful ways for young (and not so young!) professionals to advance in their careers, businesses and professional pursuits. Think of this book as a weekly field book, play book, and script to success!

To put yourself into the, "What's in it for me?" perspective and think of yourself as a time machine. Behind you is the past and in front of you is the future. Where you stand at any given time is your present tense!

The meaning of this is simple. No matter how good, bad, right or wrong, you are where you are because of the choices you have made in your past tense. These choices have driven you to where you are in your present tense, and now you are about to determine how your future will be!

Circumstances don't just happen
they happen because of the choices you make!!!

So go ahead and ask What's in it for me, if you do consider those around you in pursuit of success, ask What's in it for us. You know your psychology is going to pose these questions to you anyway, so go ahead and ask. Then make the calculated explosive choice regarding how best to advance from your present tense to the future you desire.

If you don't know what some of those choices could be, here are fifty-two of the most explosive things that you can do as gleaned from the most successful around you!

Consider one idea a week and apply each one all week throughout the entire year, and this book will serve as a play book of 52 chapters, or 52 action plans, for greater success. If you are a fast tracker, read and apply all of these ideas as fast as you can.

What's in it for me to tune in to how to advance in my career and do so with a dual mentality of aiding others around me?" A lot!

A survey released in 2003 by Challenger, Gray & Christmas, a Chicago-based employment research firm (*SUCCESSFUL Meetings* magazine March 2003 edition), revealed an estimated 3.3 million people lost their jobs in the past year. In other words, an estimated 275,000 people lost their jobs each month. With the loss of personnel in the work place, the remainder of the work has to be absorbed by the survivors. Some organizational psychologists refer to this as "ghost work".

Compounding this history, and, thus, opportunity for the young worker to be tuning in and tuning up his or her frequencies, the Bureau of Labor Statistics notes that 19 percent of the baby boomers in upper-level career positions are expected to retire within the next five years!

That is 12,480 openings or opportunities for the young career jockey each day!

These numbers are even more alarming for the public sector, where it is estimated that nearly 71 percent of workers will be eligible for retirement by 2005!

What's in it for me: As a young professional, how you position and market yourself has a direct correlation to your success in life. In fact, the bottom line is, using these fifty-two strategies, tactics and how-to action plans will directly impact your What's in it for me. A recent study in USA TODAY Newspaper for The Bernard Haldane Associates Internet Job Report, conducted by Taylor Nelson Sofres Intersearch, revealed just how workers found their current job: Networking/Word of Mouth (61 percent); Newspaper Advertisements (16 percent); Walk in/Applied in Person (9 percent); Newspaper Website (5 percent); Internet Job Site (4 percent); Employment Agency/Recruiter (2 percent); and Through School (1 percent).

With these explosive "What's in it for me" and "What's in it for us" strategies, you can greatly enhance your networking and word-of-mouth stock value with others!

One
Understanding Success Via the "X-Factor" Model©

No matter how you define success, that is the *"X-Factor"*!

"What's in it for me?" (WIIFM) typically plays off of where a person finds his or her deepest level of conviction. This is the *"Well Of Greatness©"* from which one draws. One's *"Well"* is that place deep within where one finds his or her greatest passion, emotional buy-in, conviction, strength, energy, knowledge, experience, training and abilities. It is that place where, when one arrives, going to bed at night is an inconvenience, and waking at 4 a.m. is a reality.

No matter how your define success, only a small percentage of individuals ever attain true success. Those who do ask the "What's in it for me" question continually. In asking, they are really asking "What's in it for me" in respect to how they can draw from their *"Wells"* and attain absolute peak performance within that endeavor.

For example, apply athletics to the *"X-Factor©"* formula. Imagine, what the percentage is of high school athletes who are successful enough to ascend to the collegiate level and play. Then imagine the percentage who can ascend from college and successfully play that sport at the professional level.

What percentages came to your mind? Were the numbers not greater than 10 percent and no smaller than one percent? If so, at the most liberal response of 10 percent, one is defining these individuals that have identified that at which they excel and are successful at doing. They have then pursued those opportunities and circles of influence.

Conversely, while the majority of individuals who do not fit into the successful 10 percent may be nice as people, if you drop (as mentioned in the *Preface*) the last four letters in the word "success", you arrive at the location where the majority of individuals land.

WIIFM plays to your *"X-Factor©"*, and that places you into your *"Well Of Greatness©"*. You will, therefore, avoid those tasks, jobs, and situations in which you truly do "suc"!

Two
Become an Intrapreneurial Person

Just as an entrepreneur is someone who looks outward to the market and finds a new way of spinning a service or product that fulfills a need, so too is an intrapreneurial person.

Look deep within your own *"Well Of Greatness©"* (see Chapter One) and evaluate if there are any hidden treasures. If these treasures were revealed in your present organization, would they fulfill a WIIFM growth opportunity?

If so, bring them and play them, as that is a root WIIFM variable!

Three
Expand Your Job
Responsibilities

Once you are on the inside of an organization, business, or partnership, it is time to look for ways to expand your job to play to your interests, desires, greater abilities, and expertise. If you can bring greater value (increased productivity or profitability) to others, you will find that you are answering the old "What's in it for me?" question before others even raise it!

Make yourself the resident come-to person by becoming the subject matter expert in the areas of your interest and expertise (skills, knowledge, ability, certifications, degrees, innovations, etc.).

Look for market trends and developing business units that may give insight into the best direction in which to expand. Find out who the movers-and-shakers within your organization or industry are; they will provide clues, and you will see if they excite the "What's in it for me" question.

Four
Build Alliances with the Power
Of Rule 80-10-10©

Engaging others with the "rule 80-10-10©" will raise your stock value with them. This will play to your advantage as they determine whether to associate with you or not.

To manipulate people better (of course it sounds nicer to say manage, lead, or engage others) you must recognize that when you engage individuals who have come together in a group there will be a group-think mentality. Sociology affords you a powerful model for looking at any group and designing a winning interaction model.

"Rule 80-10-10©" indicates that, while people change from subject to subject and personalities within a group change, all people within a group tend to fall into one of three distinct subgroups.

The influencers, or transformers, in any group interaction are the 10-percenters; the 80-percenters will always be the followers of the influencers.

The positive transformers of the followers are merely 10 percent of the overall group at the outset. The pessimists are terrorists to the transformers, this group is also 10 percent in power (always remember that within a group dynamic, you are merely one percent of the overall group at the outset).

To recruit a transformer to your cause and gain aid in pulling the followers along, thereby shutting down the terrorists, you must play to his or her "What's in it for me" factor. To recruit a transformer, play to him or her in advance in one of two ways:

1. People connections – who likes you, who you like, or who owes you a favor.

2. Issue connections – based upon position (age, race, gender, title, corporate position, etc.), who has the most to gain from your idea?

By enrolling transformers on your side before engaging entire groups, the victory you seek within your own "What's in it for me" factor often will be attained. You will find this is a much easier way to build alliances in your personal and professional life!

Five
Cross-Learn....

Why cross-learn? Simple...employment and independence, of which at least one is important to the young professional today!

The more diverse your skill base is, acquired by learning aggressively and thoroughly from those around you, the more options you will have available to you. The more one cross-learns, the more valuable they become to themselves and others!

Six
Networking & Personal Tagline

Imagine that you step into an elevator. The doors shut, and the person next to you asks, "Who are you?" or "What do you do?"

Being able to respond to these questions in a matter of seconds in such a way that it compels the other person to inquire to hear more is what a powerful personal tagline is!

What is your personal tagline? In Stephen Covey's classic, *Seven Habits Of Highly Successful People*, he points to the concept that successful people have personal mission statements. From your tagline or personal mission statement, you can determine with better perspective the answer to "What's in it for me" when engaging other people or situations.

If you were to take a business, for example, and print out your personal tagline, it should identify:

1. Who am I?
2. What do I stand for?

One's ability to converse with others is a large "What's in it for me" door opener called networking. Whether at a social event, business meeting, conference, or checkout line, your ability to meet, engage, and cause the other person to dialogue with you will afford you greater associations from which greater opportunities may come your direction.

A great conversation-starter could be asking the above questions to solicit a person's tagline or, even better, asking the other person open-ended questions like, "What brings you here?"

Network within nine areas of your life, and you will ensure a well-based network of contacts, advocates, and opportunities from which you will be able to draw later for your needs. Consider the following areas of your life as networking opportunities:

1. Professional
2. Family
3. Community
4. Financial
5. Inspirational
6. Social
7. Health
8. Education
9. Spiritual

"What's in it for me?" Great question. There must be balance in who one is and how one interacts with others.

In fact, in a study (F. Luthans, "Successful vs. Effective Real Managers", Academy of Management Executive, May 1988, pp. 127 – 132 and/or F. Luthans, R. M. Hodgetts, and S. A. Rosenkrantz, Real Managers [Cambridge, MA: Ballinger, 1988.]) released in the late 1990s of measurable differences between "effective managers" and "successful managers" a powerful activity differential was:

1. Effective Managers spent as much as 11 percent of their time in Networking activities (socializing, interacting with outsiders, politics, etc.).

2. Successful Managers invested as much as 48 percent of their time in Networking activities (socializing, interacting with outsiders, politics, etc.).

Seven
Request Feedback With Action Plans

Create an open dialogue with those around you – peers, subordinates, and superiors – whereby if any wish to give you feedback (positive or critical), you welcome it. Hold them accountable for sharing with you action plans on how to overcome a challenge or problem and ensure a success can be replicated!

By doing this, you will be able to manage your emotions and become less defensive and resistant to others. They will see you as a professional who is oriented towards success.

This will aid you in creating relationships with others that will allow you to convert future advocates, solicit free consultation on a daily basis, and attain greater success!

The bottom line? Requesting action plans from everyone gives you a degree of verbal or written feedback, allowing you to turn the universe into your free coaching team.

Eight
Offer Feedback With Action Plans

Create an open dialogue with those around you – peers, subordinates, and superiors – whereby if you are requested to provide feedback or you feel compelled to volunteer feedback (positive or critical), you will always share with them several action plans on how to overcome a challenge or problem and ensure a success can be replicated!

By doing so, you will avoid the dreaded perception that many young people are negative and critical at all times and never have a resolution or solution.

Also, you will attain greater success, attract more support networks from others, and increase your stock value in the minds of others!

Nine
Volunteer Internally
Strategically

Determine where you want to be going in your present life. When you've figured it out, use that as a benchmark for volunteering for internal activities, committees, special projects, etc.

If upward mobility is a desire, volunteering internally for opportunities that will allow you to engage the power brokers is smart. Conversely, toiling away on labor-intense activities that others will present to the power brokers may be unwise, as others will ascend because of your efforts!

Ten
Identify "Gaps-n-Cracks"

Here is another power clue that will always bring you greater success, ...

Evaluate which products, services, and deliverables your organization is missing right now. Address the influencers, stating you have a way of addressing that gap or crack and, thus, creating greater opportunities.

By doing so, not only do you become the winner of the day, but you attain your desired goal by doing the things you want and getting paid for them!

Eleven
Identify One Percent Factors©

Your body will resist most major changes in behavior or action if it fails to see the WIIFM of the change.

However, you typically will not even process changing your behavior if the adjustment or change involves a mere 1 percent adjustment!

So, instead of looking at just a few things you can change significantly to achieve success, look for the little things that yield significant growth. The WIIFM of this is that it will require less energy and produce greater results.

Twelve
Dress

If it looks like a duck, walks like a duck, and sounds like a duck, it's a duck!

That adage has direct application to you as an individual. People begin to judge you before they ever meet you. So look in a mirror and ask yourself what message your wardrobe emits. Is it portraying an accurate representation of who you are? If not, there is a clue – change.

A very successful woman once said, "You don't dress for the job you have, you dress for the job you want."

In fact, a few years ago there was a study by Adia Temporary Services that revealed a time lapse of typically seven seconds between when two people first see each other and when the first words and/or handshake are exchanged. In those seven seconds, impressions are being formulated based solely upon one's dress, the Seven Second Rule!

The WIIFM factor is that you may be building walls instead of creating doorways through which you can access success. Your dress leaves a strong impression with people . . . it may not be fair, but it is reality!

.

Thirteen
Mirror Effectively

Learn how to read others and adjust your persona to blend, equal, or mirror them. This causes people to feel more comfortable around you and increases the desire of others to want to be in your space.

Example: While in the deep southern states in America, you may slow your speech pace. Conversely, in New York City you would increase your speech pace. Both are examples of mirroring.

By mirroring others, they will connect with you more readily and thus your interaction effectiveness will skyrocket.

Ways to mirror effectively and quickly are:

1. Pace
2. Tone
3. Volume of speech
4. Types of words used
5. Posture
6. Eye contact

Fourteen
Learn to Forecast

Hindsight is 20-20. More than just another adage, this statement is powerful.

As a tuned-in and turned-on participant in the organizations with which you associate, become observant to that which goes on around you. When you recognize something that may result in a different and more desirable outcome, share that knowledge as early as possible with all vested parties. In other words, forecast!

Forecast based upon sound data and not possible emotional problems, difficulties, short falls, technology issues, labor challenges, etc. You will see things on the front side of an engagement, giving you time to make calculated adjustments to avoid negativity and problems and to attain greater success.

Fifteen
Cultivate Advocates Externally

An advocate is a person who serves as your surrogate marketer, champion, public relations agent, and sales representative when you are not present to "blow your own horn"!

An advocate is someone who knows you, believes in you, respects you, is well positioned within his or her community or industry, and has a deep circle of influence. An advocate is a person who has a following and knows how to shorten your success race, thus aiding you in greater victories.

Having such a person outside of where you immediately work and live is the intent of an "external advocate". The more advocates you have, the more rewards, awards, and door-opening opportunities you will experience.

Sixteen
Cultivate Advocates Internally

An advocate is a person who serves as your surrogate marketer, champion, public relations agent, and sales representative when you are not present to "blow your own horn"!

An advocate is someone who knows you, believes in you, respects you, is well positioned within your mutual community, industry, or organization, and has a deep circle of influence. An advocate is a person who has a following and knows how to shorten your success race, thus aiding you in greater victories.

Having such a person inside of where you immediately work and live is the intent of an "internal advocate". The more advocates you have, the more rewards, awards, and door-opening opportunities you will experience.

"Internal advocates" serve as buffers against potential negative attacks on you when you're absent. They also serve to navigate you to greater internal opportunities.

Seventeen
Integrate Strategically into Teams

Recognize that people are often judged by the company they keep. The adage "Birds of a feather flock _____" is profound!

When you arrive on site to a new team, department, or group, avoid being seen as standoffish. At the same time, however, be judicious in how you go about engaging these new people (review Chapter Four).

Be guarded in how quickly you confide in people and in whom you confide. Remember another powerful adage, "Loose lips sink____!"

You should test the waters of confidentiality. If you choose to share confidential information with others, start with low-level information and observe the actions of everyone involved. You will be able to determine if the confidence has been honored or violated.

It is best to integrate strategically into a team and have a low-level "oops", rather than a major implosion!

Eighteen
Vertical Action Information Gram©

What is a *Vertical Action Information Gram©*?

Whether done verbally or sent as an e-mail, letter or fax, the intent is to briefly recap and share with your boss all of your victories and major accomplishments in a given period of time.

Most often, bosses are informed of problems and negativity. Here, we raise our stock value to others by associating productivity and profitability gains with our name.

You can enhance this even further. If, for example, these gains were accomplished in concert with the efforts of others (peers or colleagues from other business operating units), ensure that you send a copy to all of their bosses, thereby raising their stock value through your initiative. A bounce-back bonus might be that these other bosses are impressed with your residual efforts as well.

Determine if the application of this technique is best for your work environment when done daily, weekly, monthly, etc. Once this has been determined, continue on a regular and consistent basis.

Nineteen
Horizontal Action Information Gram©

What is a *Horizontal Action Information Gram©*?

Whether done verbally or sent as an e-mail, letter or fax, the intent is to briefly recap and share with your peers all of your victories and major accomplishments in a given period of time.

Most often, your colleagues only hear about problems and negativity. Here, we raise our stock value to others by associating productivity and profitability gains with our name.

You can enhance this even further. If, for example, these gains were accomplished in concert with the efforts of others (peers or colleagues from other business operating units), ensure that you send a copy to all of their colleagues, thereby raising their stock value through your initiative. A bounce-back bonus might be that these other colleagues are impressed with your residual efforts as well.

Determine if the application of this technique is best for your work environment when done daily, weekly, monthly, etc. Once this has been determined, continue on a regular and consistent basis.

Twenty
Volunteer Externally Strategically

Determine where it is you want to be going in your present life. Once that is determined, use that location as a benchmark for volunteering for external activities, clubs, associations, church groups, civic groups, community events, special projects, etc.

If upward mobility is a desire, volunteering externally for opportunities that will allow you to engage the power brokers is smart. Conversely, toiling away on labor-intense activities that others will present to the power brokers may be unwise, as they will garner the spotlight because of your efforts!

To grow your leadership ability, uncover your hidden talents, and accentuate your abilities to greatness, look for ways to learn, grow, develop, showcase your talents, and network with other like-minded performers. Consider joining:

1. The United States Junior Chamber (US Jaycees) with a mission of building tomorrow's leaders today, at www.USJaycees.org.

2. The Association of Junior Leagues International at www.ajli.org, "Women building better communities".

Twenty-One
Invest in Yourself & Share Strategically Weekly

Play a simple game of math and money to see how you have been conditioned to value yourself. Hint: think of a monthly number for each of the following questions, then simply multiple by twelve to arrive at your final answer.

1. In the past year, how much money would you estimate you have spent on your hair (maintenance, hair care products, etc.)? $_____

2. In the past year, how much money would you estimate you have spent on your face (maintenance, face care products, etc.)? $_____

3. In the past year, how much money would you estimate you have spent on your wardrobe (maintenance, cleaning, new purchases, etc.)? $_____

Add up those three numbers, representing the amount of money you invest in yourself, to project the outward image you feel is important.

With that total number established, let's consider a fourth question. More than likely, it is the most important number you will ever recognize if you truly wish to attain greatness outside of Hollywood.

4. In the past year, how much money would you estimate you have spent on your head (what you

have put into your head and how you have added to your head)? $_____

That which is within your head will serve as the engine that propels the outward body that others see. The greater your skill and intellectual assets are, the greater will be your ability to invest in others on a weekly basis.

By doing so, your personal power, influence, and stock value will rise greatly!

Twenty-Two
Always Make the Boss Look Good

You can respect them, care for them, admire them, disagree with them, and even dislike them. Whatever the sentiments may be, the reality is that your boss still signs your paycheck!

You can have healthy issue-oriented disagreements in private and in meetings, but when you go out of that domain and into the public eye of the organization, your success within that environment is still tied to the relationship you have with your boss.

What's in it for me is answered in whether or not you desire to remain employed within that organization.

Always make your boss look good with what you do and say.

Twenty-Three
Identify Your USFX2©

The marketing world suggests that organizations can differentiate themselves in a market and attain greater market share by evaluating their USF factor. We will give a second interpretation of the standard USF factor to afford you two ways to increase your stock value with others!

1. USF #1 represents the *Unique Selling Feature* (or the "What" factor) that you offer, sell, or provide to others.

2. USF #2 represents the *Unique Service Feature* (or the "How" factor), which implies the way you uniquely deliver the USF #1.

Your ability to determine the quantity of ways in which you can communicate to others your USF #1 or USF #2 that is actually different than others', results in increasing your value to others.

A powerful way to differentiate is through professional certifications for the business industry that you are in or aspire towards, as well as advanced formal and informal education attainment.

Twenty-Four
Don't Smoke, Unless . . .

A real power point to success and advancing in your career is not to smoke in professional environments and situations.

Now we are not advocating a "don't smoke" policy. What we are advocating is, "Don't smoke!"

An alarming pattern of human behavior has developed when smokers gather. In these groups, the dialogue tends to center around complaining, negativity, and a wide array of problems. As one engages in such dialogue, his or her stock value stagnates or plummets in the mind's eye of others.

If you truly want to excel in life, the next time you smoke or interact with those that do, strive to maintain a positive dialogue. Even better would be to take advantage of that two to three minutes of smoke time to capitalize on a captive audience. Cultivate solution dialogue from them and convert them into your free consultants!

Twenty-Five
Get Out of the
"Presenter's Box©"

Avoiding confrontations and defense posture in the act of presenting new ideas to groups and individuals will enable you to attain greater success. That is a powerful WIIFM objective!

Every time you present an idea, topic, project, or solution, while standing in front of a group, you tend to stand firm as if you were standing within an imaginary *"Presenter's Box"*. At the moment that someone either interrupts or challenges you, typically you would stand firm, dig in, justify, explain, or even challenge them in return. This same behavior is present when you sit and present. Most people tend to lean forward at the moment they present, and when under challenge, they lean firmly forward.

The longer one remains in the box, the greater the likelihood is of implosion.

By removing yourself from the box you maintain control of yourself and engage the other person in a controlled manner for solution outcome, thus pulling others to your cause.

The next time someone challenges you:

1. As they interrupt you, simply, slowly, and calmly step to the side of where you were, thus stepping out of the *"Presenter's Box©"*.

2. When they complete their statement, calmly gesture to the space that you had occupied and would have been defending.

3. Calmly pose a question with a constructive tone of voice. You could say, for example, "If this idea is not an effective way to proceed, let's explore some other options. What might be some other ways for us to address this issue?"

By removing yourself from the box, you can remain forward focused!

Twenty-Six
Communicate Only in
"Safe Zones©"

Avoid torpedoing yourself – don't open your mouth unless you are in a *"safe zone"!*

A *"safe zone"* is a place where you are sure NO ONE CAN HEAR YOU. The number of people who are overheard gossiping, complaining, and talking about strategic internal business and proprietary information is staggering. From Fortune 500 executives and entrepreneurs to religious leaders and association members, if you "talk shop", as they say, make sure NO ONE IS NEAR.

The next time you are seated in a restaurant talking, consider who is in the next booth, at the next table, or on the other side of a curtain or wall, who can hear your every word. When you are on an elevator, who is standing off to the side, listening intently and taking mental notes to be shared with others without your knowledge?

Twenty-Seven
Zero Sum Confidentiality

When in doubt, shut up!

You may have individuals in your personal and professional life in whom you wish to confide or who approach you to confide in them. Before you choose to do so, however, ask yourself two powerful questions:

1. In whom do they confide?

2. Do I have any reason to trust them?

Most people fail to realize that the characteristics of the one in whom they confide may not be congruent with THAT person's confidant.

In business, people do not always play by the rules of confidentiality, ethics, and integrity. So be sure you play by the CYA model . . .cover your actions!

Twenty-Eight
Psychology of Others ... Speed-Reading Personalities/Social Styles

Your ability to understand that certain people think, operate, respond, and engage others based upon their personality/social style preferences will prove invaluable to your pursuits.

To speed-read a personality or social style, look at the totality of the person's actions, behavioral patterns and language at any given time. Measure those observations (data points) against two basic variables.

Visualize a plus sign. On the vertical axis, score from high to low any indicators of the other person's (or yourself for that matter, if you were assessing yourself to determine your dominant professional or personal personality/social style) comfort zone.

A high score would be defined as a tendency or desire for more structure, formality, concise communication exchanges, etc. A low score would be defined as the opposite desire for less structure, informality, casualness, more communication, etc.

Now with that plus sign graph, measure on the horizontal axis a person's energy zone.

On the right side of the horizontal axis are those with energy tendencies that are fast, outgoing, assertive, aggressive, not very patient, and easily stressed. Leftward tendencies are seen as more patient, methodical, calculating, analytical, and not as easily stressed.

By scoring yourself and others on the two lines and finding their meeting points, you will land in one of the four quadrants imposed by the plus sign model. Determining your quadrant personality behaviors allows you to become more receptive to moving into others' quadrants and engaging them from their perspective.

Top right quadrant personalities tend to be more of a Driver/Type "A". Bottom right quadrant personalities tend to be more of an Expressive/Coach. Bottom left quadrant personalities tend to be an Amiable/Blender. Top left quadrant personalities tend to be more of an Analytical/Thinker.

Understanding this will aid you in communicating with others in the manner in which each prefers to operate.

The "What's in it for me" factor is easier interactions, reduced conflicts, and passive-aggressive behavior situations. That correlates into greater success for everyone!

(For more information and understanding on personalities and instruments for plotting yours and others personality/social styles, get your copy of Building A Legendary Leader [ISBN # 0-9718010-2 /US $29.95 JMI Publishers] and YIELD MANAGEMENT, by CRC Press [ISBN# 1-57444-206-6 /USA $29.95]. To see other exciting resource books and audio and video titles, go to www.JeffreyMagee.com/Library.asp)

Twenty-Nine
Rule 1/12/50© & eApplications

Staying connected with your advocates, associates, and close friends can become time consuming and, is thereford considered a "project" to most.

Here is a simple technique that yields high results. It can be used in business for increased productivity and profitability, as well as in one's personal life for increased success.

Be diligent in doing this like clock work (hence the #1) the first part of every month (hence the #12). Identify upwards of 50 people (hence the #50) who you want to inform about a new accomplishment, promotion, or service of which they may not be aware. If you were in a sales position, for example, these would be 50 potential customers that you would, for matriculation purposes, need to follow up with either in person or via the telephone.

Thirty
Compete With the One Who Counts

Far too many people compete against unfair forces, which causes an eventual implosion. With that said, whom do most people compete with and whom should you compete with in reality? Consider these forces:

1. Some compete against someone else.

2. Some compete against something else.

3. Some compete against apathy or nothing else.

Amazingly, what we should be competing with is none of these forces. Rather, WIIFM is to compete with:

1. Our positive self.

2. Our negative self.

Keeping in touch with one's optimism and keeping that grounded will aid in propelling you forward faster!

Keeping your pessimism in check will aid in avoiding implosion and reducing self-imposed negativity.

Always compete with the powerful forces that lie within you and only you. Always live up to your imposed performance bar of excellence!

Thirty-One
Mentor Engagement & Five
Levels of Success

You can learn from others on five levels and grow others on five levels. Here is a powerful five level mentor engagement model for success:

1. *Elementary Mentor* provides basic knowledge and education to another person. If you lack even the elementary knowledge on a subject, you need to seek out a person who is patient, knowledgeable, and willing to grow you. If you are sincere in your approach, people will share openly and graciously.

2. *Secondary Mentor* expands upon basic knowledge and ensures, through repetition, you know how to truly apply the knowledge and skills.

3. *Post-Secondary Mentor* guides one possessing the fundamental knowledge and skills into multiple applications of usage of that knowledge. This mentor also has the ability to guide the use of that knowledge in various directions inside and outside an organization.

4. *Master Mentor* has deep connections within your industry, organization, and community. He or she serves as your advocate to others when you least expect it and don't expect it. This mentor can make opportunities happen for you and navigate you toward greater success in life.

5. *Reverse Mentor* has progressed from being in the hands of an Elementary Mentor through a Master Mentor. Now you have earned the right to grow others in the discipline you have mastered!

Raising your stock value by learning from others and growing others should speak to your "What's in it for me factor".

Thirty-Two
Craft Your Resume Monthly

WIIFM ("What's in it for me factor") is a great benchmark for every thing you do. Consider the drill of creating or updating your resume monthly and the information it would provide.

Under education, you can evaluate any workshops, seminars, conferences, certifications, or degrees you have attended or attained. Is there anything new to add or does each month reveal that your educational attainment equals that of an amoeba?

Under work experience, have you added to that diverse platform of accomplishments and tasks you have undertaken, been held accountable for, and experienced? Or does this month's section on your resume resemble the previous month?

"What's in it for me factor?" Simple. If your resume today resembles that of two months ago, you are stagnant and being unemployed is what you deserve.

Continual growth in these two fields on your monthly resume leads to greater success!

Thirty-Three
Plant Lots of TRES©

Imagine plant only one type of tree in an orchard. Then a parasite which only feeds off your trees comes through. You are out of business.

The same holds true if all of your skills are too similar or if you have all of your contacts and associations in too narrow of an area.

Borrowing a term from the military, your *TRE* is your *"Target Rich Environment".*

Look for those places, people, and things that add value to and complement your present efforts. When you find them, add them to your life, thus planting lots of *TREs* for greater success. Look into every *TRE* you plant and identify within it as many branches of contacts as you can. Ensure that you get to know all of them and they get to know you!

Thirty-Four
E-mail Distribution List Management

The power lies within whom you know, how easily you can retrieve a date, and knowing how to use and flex that date to your advantage!

Having a fluid database management system – in which you can collect people's names, addresses, phone numbers, and fax numbers, as well as maintain infinite notes and e-mail addresses for easy contact and communication via electronic newsletters, chat rooms, and online dialogues – places you into a position of power.

Information is power, and the effective use of that information is success!

Thirty-Five
Use the "Player Capability Index©" for Assessment and Growth

People are subjective creatures at heart. An instrument that aids in critical objectivity can only aid an individual in attaining growth and greater success. This ability is powerful in guiding the development of those around you and determining how to assign or volunteer for tasks.

The *"Player Capability Index©"* is a human resource analysis instrument which allows an individual to truly determine what one is capable of by tapping deep into what one possesses.

The model:

$$C \ \frac{T2+A+P}{E2} = R$$

To determine the net results (hence the R) of that of which you are capable (hence the C) go inside the formula. The T represents Training, and the 2 represents Two Interpretations. First, you must evaluate the totality of training you have received from birth to today. If you lack the T necessary to be C of generating the needed R, the second interpretation would be the additional training that you need. The A represents one's Attitude, which drives how one will or will not draw upon his or her T for any given situation. The P represents Performance, which reflects how one has done and will do things. It is the quality of someone's P that is influenced by both their expectations and those of the other party (hence the E) which drives the C that dictates the R.

When confronted with a task, project, or endeavor (R), process the R to determine the level C a successful candidate must possess for success!

Thirty-Six
Become Proficient with
D=C+L

The more you improve as a communicator (C = the art and science of sending a communication signal) and an active listener (L = the art and science of receiving a communication signal), the richer your dialogues (D) will become with others.

If you want others to gravitate toward you and engage in healthy dialogue, you must be an aggressive student and practitioner of communication and listening!

Thirty-Seven
Self-Business Cards

Your business card is your personal billboard on the highway of life. If your employer, business, or organization does not offer them, get one!

Your business card is your statement of professionalism, which says, "I have arrived!"

Your business card should tell others in a powerful and clear manner:

1. Your name

2. Your phone, fax, and e-mail contact data

3. Your physical or postal mailing address

4. Your vocation, occupation, and status for which you want to be known

5. Your credentials

Your business card should always be:

1. In your wallet

2. In your briefcase

3. In your day planner or PDA case

4. In your car

5. In your work space

You never know when you will need to give your card to someone as a solution provider for a need they have. Plus, you might need to use it to detail specific information on the reverse side, thus converting your business card into a mobile note card or tailored proposal to give to someone.

Always have your self-business card, as it says, "Here is who I am, and here is how I can make your life better!"

Thirty-Eight
Hotel Sleeping Rooms Stationery
& the Magic of Threes

Open any quality hotel room desk drawer and you will find a blotter with stationery and envelopes. If you count the sheets of stationery and envelopes, it seems to be a phenomenon that there are always three sheets and three envelopes.

Always make it a mission to take those three sheets out and draft a short note to someone (your advocates, family members, friends, or even a client). Share with them your travels, where you are, what you are doing, or simply something that could enrich their quality of life.

By doing so your stock value rises.

Replicate this model at home with your own stationery, personalized note cards, or business letterhead. Studies indicate that hand written notes are valued more and read quicker than printed messages.

Thirty-Nine
Mistakes

Learn from the mistakes of others because you will never live long enough to make them all yourself. There are so many mistakes you see in your life each and every day. Why not learn from them and remember the lessons?

What is one of the best ways to learn how to do something? Watch someone else do it, do it yourself, and have the ability to effectively teach someone else how to do it. The whole basis of being able to teach a concept to someone else is watching another person do it first. Why not use this same concept with mistakes? By simply watching and learning from others' mistakes, you can effectively eliminate many hassles and embarrassing situations from your life.

Let's take this concept one step further. How about learning from the mistakes history has shown us? How many times have you said to yourself, "That's not the first time that has ever been done", or, "I've seen this happen before"?

In the 2002 video, The Commanding Heights, produced by PBS and available online at www.pbs.org, there is a story about a Russian woman and her young son, who were living in the former Soviet Union when the Berlin Wall fell in 1989. In 2002, that same woman's son, now 19 years of age, asked his mother, "What is Marxism? What is Communism about?" WHAT? My, my, how quickly we forget. Seven decades of communism is what the former Soviet Union had as a government! If people do not learn from history, especially the mistakes of history, it is so easy for "history to repeat itself"!

Again, learn from the mistakes of others because you will never live long enough to make them all yourself.

Forty
Positive Mental Attitude

Is a positive mental attitude (PMA) really a secret to success?

Studies show that people with a PMA are more resilient to stress and live longer lives. Maybe one should reprogram one's thinking more toward "Yes, Yes, Yes" instead of "No, No, No!"

"Yes I can, Yes I can, Yes I can." is like the Sermon on the Mount, "Ask, and it shall be given you...Knock, and it shall be opened unto you."(Matthew 7:7)

Surround yourself with positive energy, positive people, and positive things, and you will be stunned by the level of success you can experience.

Conversely, limit your exposure to negative attitude feeders and they can become toxic to your success!

Negative attitudes are like cancer, and there are two choices you must make. You can keep a negative attitude and allow it to spread throughout your entire being which will, in turn, cause you much pain, grief, heart ache, loss of friends, loss of family members, etc. Or you can make the choice to cut out the cancerous negative attitude and be happy.

YES, IT IS YOUR CHOICE TO BE EITHER HAPPY OR NEGATIVE! When you wake up each and every morning, there are two questions you need to ask yourself. "Do I choose to be happy (positive)? Or do I choose to be grumpy (negative)?" Make your decision quickly and then begin your day, practicing the decision you made all day long. Changing a negative attitude to a positive attitude takes patience, discipline, and practice. It can, however, be done. Practice, practice, practice!

Digging a little deeper, you might ask yourself, "How do I ensure my thinking is as positive as possible?" Consider the application of the *FIST Factor©* as your mental Board of Directors.

Open your hand, palm up, and visualize the people (past or present) who occupy mental space and influence over how you think and feel. As you mentally see individuals, attribute one name per finger that you have extended in the flexed open hand. For each name that immediately comes to you, collapse that finger and keep the immediate inventory going. Upon initial inventory, most people doing this exercise see that they tend to have at least five people who actually do occupy this mental space, thus influencing their behaviors.

With this revelation you can recognize that, with the fingers all counted down, your open hand is transformed into a fist. This is the *FIST Factor©* where your mental power, strength, and energy force are rooted – good or bad.

A healthy and balanced successful person needs five different types of *FIST Factor©* board members. You may not have exactly five people who represent these categories, but you must have all five occupied. Any open categories are in fact just that: openings to be filled with constructive candidates.

A healthy *FIST Factor©* should have representation from:

1. Your FAMILY/PERSONAL life.

2. Your PROFESSIONAL life.
3. Your FRIEND circle of influence.
4. Your most SUCCESSFUL contact.
5. The greatest UNDERDOG you know.

Now analyze your present *FIST Factor©* and determine if any category is vacant. By having each category filled, you have greater mental points of reference for success!

Now reference Chapter Four and ensure that none of your mental Board of Directors or members of your *FIST Factor©* are members of the 80 percent Followers subgroup or 10 percent Terrorist subgroup. You will be more inclined to listen to the present members of your Board before a new person of the richness of this book. Replace both subgroups on your *FIST Factor©* if they are present with only Transformers!

Forty-One
Finances

We have all heard the parental financial advice:

"You should keep three months' worth of your salary in savings . . . invest 10 percent of every dollar you make for retirement . . . the best time to invest was yesterday!"

The number of people who actually do this is staggeringly low.

The best time to make a budget adjustment and invest in yourself is when you have a job. Recognize that you should not be doing this as you lose your job.

If you lost your job today, would it merely be an unexpected paid vacation because you have an established savings or would it be a trauma scene?

To become financially wealthy, one must <u>learn</u> how to become financially wealthy. The rich teach their kids how to create and preserve financial wealth. Those who are not brought up in this world of learning <u>must learn</u> how to create it, if and only if they have a goal and desire to become financially wealthy.

The first step to creating and preserving wealth is patience and discipline. Your financial wealth will not be created overnight. Second, you must eliminate all bad debt (i.e. credit cards and anything else you cannot pay for with cash). Third, you must learn how to have the assets you own (i.e. rental properties, owning your own business, etc.) pay for all the liabilities (taxes, bills, etc.) you have.

When I was 18 years old, my uncle Bob taught me two of the most valuable lessons I have ever learned in creating my personal financial wealth. He said, "Damon, two points in creating your own personal financial wealth are:

1. The law of compounding interest. The younger you start investing, the greater advantage you will have with compounding interest.
2. A young person should only finance (borrow money to purchase) three things in his or her life:
   a. first car
   b. education (College, Masters, PhD, etc.)
   c. first home

You should pay for everything else in cash."

Even those of us who live on very little income <u>can</u> create and preserve personal financial wealth by living by these two key points.

Forty-Two
Get Involved

Join networking groups, community groups, young professional groups (like the US Jaycees at www.USJacees.org or The Association of Junior Leagues International at www.ajli.org) or anything that will allow you to meet and build relationships with young leaders of tomorrow!

I am only assuming that you fall into the leadership category for the simple fact that you are reading this book! You are "Today's Young Leaders for Tomorrow's Future." Get involved now! One day you will inherit and effectively manage the United States trade deficit, the terrorist threat level, the world of globalization, Social Security, United States relations with our allies and other countries, your state government, your local and city government, etc.

How will you effectively and efficiently manage the society in which we all live? It's simple: by getting involved now and learning now how today's systems process, we may run the processes better in the future. Networking with the correct people will always provide you with the opportunities of a lifetime!

It is estimated that the average adult in a nonacademic environment does not read even two nonfiction books a year.

WOW! You have almost completed one, thus placing you at the average mark. If you have read other books before this one and read more after this one, you are a star in comparison to most people!

Forty-Three
Don't Gripe

It has become very fashionable and even condoned by most today to gripe, complain, point fingers, and cast blame!

Don't gripe or complain about anything. Instead, stand up and do something about it!

If you don't participate in and address that which you speak about, you have intellectually abdicated your right to voice a view. If you do not vote in an election, how can you possibly hold a conversation and offer opinions with someone who did vote? It is the same concept. If you gripe about something, but don't do anything about it, how can you justify your opinion, gripe, or complaint? You can't!

The only thing you will be doing is effectively turning people away from you and any opinions you may have. Stand up and do something about the issues about which you are passionate and vocal. This will give you the leverage necessary to effectively and efficiently defend your opinions should you be challenged.

Complaining only plays into the hands of those who say others (and especially younger people) only take and complain. Prove them incorrect with that observation!

Forty-Four
Networking

It was once referred to as brown nosing, sucking up, and being a teacher's pet. In the adult world, it is referred to as office politics, sucking up, and being a boss's pet. Of course, in the past decade, it was given a much more fashionable name – networking!

Whatever you call it, taking the opportunity to extend your hand to another, introduce yourself, and exchange business cards is the art and science of meeting others.

Sometimes it is not who you know,
BUT who knows you!

Until you know the *Five Ws and One H* of those around you, start talking. By asking controlled, open-ended questions, you may be guiding the conversation, but the other person will be dominating the conversation. During these conversations, keep in mind that the person you are talking to is 10,000 times more interested in him - or herself than they are in you. So, ask all of the *Five Ws and One H* and then some. You will soon know more about that individual than you ever thought you would want to know.

Networking groups allow you to meet the movers and shakers of your community. These people will begin to know who you are if you drop your pride barriers and approach and introduce yourself first. I love the saying, "Sometimes it is not about what you know, but who you know." I love even better to take this saying one step further, "Sometimes it is not who <u>you</u> know, BUT <u>who</u> knows you!"

WIIFM? The more you know about others, the greater your success will be.

Forty-Five
Time for Yourself

You need to be heart healthy, mind healthy, and relationship healthy.

People are like finely-tuned pieces of machinery, and they need some self-preventative maintenance time. Studies show that when a person goes on a vacation, his or her productivity and proficiency skyrockets upon return.

Take time for yourself…at least 30 minutes a day. You want it anyway, so why not budget for it?

1. Read
2. Walk
3. Exercise
4. Spend time with animals or nature
5. Watch a sunset
6. Walk on a beach
7. Hike in the mountains
8. Walk in a grassy field and listen to the birds
9. Watch relaxing television or a movie
10. Listen to relaxing music
11. Look at old letters and photographs that recall good memories
12. Write or do a crossword puzzle
13. Talk casually with others
14. Take a hot bath
15. Engage in a hobby

Enough said!

Forty-Six
Marketing

Think of anything you want to do or accomplish. All of the activities that go into positioning you for the potential of getting what you want are what marketing is all about.

What is the best form of marketing? Word-of-mouth!!! If you remember to always keep a positive mental attitude, treat others as you would want to be treated, and have a product from which people will benefit, more times than not the word-of-mouth marketing you receive from your customers will be awesome!

Having trouble getting that key appointment? Want to make a fun, original, but lasting first impression? Try sending prospects or future business partners a handwritten postcard with a beautiful picture of a tropical island! That will not only grab their attention but will give them a short sensation of joy! Beautiful pictures of mountains, beaches, oceans, sunsets, trees, animals, etc. always quickly grab the attention of humans, thus taking them to a place they look forward to being. It is an instant gratification feeling that might grab them during a hectic and stressful time of their day. It is definitely a positive way to make a lasting first impression.

I have heard of people who use the postcard marketing concept who actually receive phone calls from the prospective client or future business partner because of the beautiful picture with the handwritten note. It's a new concept, it's a fun concept, and it's a concept that works!

The message that you market, convey, or telegraph to others is the message by which they score or judge you. In fact this *"Judgment by Association©"* transcends to your networking activities, resume, USF and how others advocate you or avoid you!

Forty-Seven
Rules of Engagement

Understanding how people play and how to successfully interact with them is the clue one gains by understanding the Rules of Engagement.

In what industry do you reside, in what industry do you want to reside, or in what industry does your new and improved product fit? Find out!

There are lots of rules and regulations. Rules of engagement can be seen all around us. Whether within personal relationships, within the workplace, or within the community, rules of engagement become the blueprint for successful interactions!

For example, in considering the rules of engagement for international business success, an understanding of globalization would be necessary. Breaking down the barriers to trade of the international markets, thus creating the most effective possible means of selling goods and services, would be a definition or rule of engagement for globalization.

Learning how to play by the *rules of engagement* is absolutely key in any country where you do business and with each person with whom you connect. Consider how many engagement rules you presently know about:

1. Your immediate supervisor, boss, leader where you work.
2. Your best customer.
3. Your spouse, partner, parents, siblings, children.

4. Your sibling's spouse or partners.
5. Your colleagues at work.
6. Your friends, neighbors, colleagues within the associations or organizations that you participate in outside of work.
7. Etc.

Forty-Eight
Knowledge of All Generations

Having a greater understanding and working knowledge of ALL generations you will come into contact with today, tomorrow, and in your future will have a direct influence on your success.

It is not a matter of right versus wrong or good versus bad; it is merely a working reality. The reality is that today's workplace is made up of five different generational segmentations, each operating from a different perspective.

There are Centurions (55 and older), Baby Boomers (38-to 55-year-olds), Generation X'ers (28-to 38-year-olds), Generation Y'ers (22-to 28-year-olds) and MTV'ers (17-to 22-year-olds).

The more you know about the other person, client, or competitor in respect to their generational segmentation, the more ahead of the game you will be (A great book on generational engagement and leadership is, *COACHING FOR IMPACT: Leadership and the Art of Generational Coaching*©. Go to www.JeffreyMagee.com/Library.asp to order your copy today!)

While most people are still engaged in evaluating people based solely upon gender and race, there are greater influence opportunities based upon how one's psychology shapes behavior (generational segmentation).

Successful managers and business owners understand how and why each generational segment behaves the way they do. Because of this knowledge, these successful managers and business owners can effectively influence the outcomes of behaviors and change the performance of the organization by effectively making their employees happy and their businesses successful.

Remember, employees are the lifeblood of a company. Employees can either "make" a company successful or "break" a company, forcing that organization into bankruptcy. Successful managers and business owners know this. Their employees are treated like family, thus making the business successful.

Forty-Nine
Trust in a Supreme Being

Trust in a Something that gives you grounding in your daily routine.

Faith is a big portion of what life is all about. You must have something higher in your life that you feel supports you. Human needs and desires from other humans are very important, but the human needs and desires from a Supreme Being are just as important. What is your faith based upon, and how often do you go back to it?

Refer to Chapter 40 and the Sermon on the Mount: "Ask, and it shall be given you ... knock, and it shall be opened unto you." This Supreme Being should only be a positive influence in your life. If there is any negativity associated with the "something higher in your life," you must immediately find out why and what is the source of this negativity. Then immediately oust it from your life!

Successful individuals do not allow negativity to control their lives. They have learned how to effectively and efficiently deal with negativity.

Fifty
Trust in Yourself & Challenge Yourself

Trust in your natural abilities because we all have them! What are your natural abilities? Don't know? Ask someone you trust. Sometimes we need guidance from others who are looking at us from the outside before we can realize who we are and what natural abilities we have. Other times, we just know what our natural abilities are because we know that we know that we know!

Once you discover your natural abilities, develop them by practicing what you are good at. Music, business, computers, running, skiing, medicine, singing, acting, writing, politics, flying, leading, mentoring…whatever it is, trust in it!

If you can't trust in yourself, whom can you trust? One of my favorite quotes is from former President Ronald Reagan: "If not now, when? If not us, who?" POWERFUL! Ask yourself, "If not now, when? If not me, who?"

You have to trust in yourself to become successful. You have to trust in yourself before you can trust others. It takes practice and time, but I trust and believe you can do it!

Fifty-One
Ask Questions & Travel

Ask questions, ask questions, ask questions. Don't be afraid to ask questions of the people who are already successful. You just may learn something!

Always ask as many questions as possible. I learned the "balloon full of air" theory from my mentor and best friend, Paul Wheeler, President and Owner of Accent Realtors, www.accentrealtors.com, and fellow young professional!

When you meet someone in person or talk to someone on the phone for the first time, they may be like a "balloon full of air". The "Air" represents stress. They are fragile, quick to react to anything, and can easily burst if the wrong thing is said or done. Once you start asking lots of key questions, the "balloon full of air" starts to release pressure and stress. Soon the balloon is deflated enough that the person is no longer fragile and quick to react.

Again, remember that people are 10,000 times more interested in themselves than they are in you. If you ask lots of key questions about them, they will feel that you have a key interest in who they are, therefore releasing the pressure and stress of the "balloon full of air".

Travel, travel, travel. Another excellent way to take time for yourself and educate yourself about this wonderful world we live in is to get out and travel!

Go far! Go wide! Go deep! See as much as you can!

We all have powerful points of reference upon which we can draw for greater success. Your ability to tune backward and into the "What's in it for me factor" of the past may greatly serve you in the present for greater success in your future.

For example, I (Damon) was very fortunate as a child because my mother got me a volunteer position at the zoo where I lived, The Tulsa Zoo and Living Museum, www.tulsazoo.org.

Although I was not traveling to places like Africa and Asia, I was learning firsthand at age 12 what kind of power a one-and-a-half-year-old baby Asian Elephant truly has! From the ages of 12 to 18, I was involved in a program called Zoo Teens. The program gave teenagers the opportunity to work with and shadow a paid zookeeper. I had a personal interest in primates and large mammals. Working with, feeding, and cleaning up after Maverick, the one-and-a-half-year-old baby Asian elephant, was a personal and educational experience I will have for the rest of my life.

Do you know the most distinctive feature difference between Asian and African elephants? The ears. The African elephants' ears are much larger than the Asian elephants' ears.

Why am I telling you about this childhood experience of mine? Because although at the ages of 12 to 18 I was not physically traveling to Asia and Africa, I have <u>educational</u> experiences of both continents that you can usually only receive from traveling there. This childhood experience, along with many more Tulsa Zoo stories, has prompted me in my young adult years to get out, travel, and learn what this small world we live in is all about.

Traveling is the best education anyone can have!

On your resume under your "Accomplishments and Achievements" section (see Chapter Thirty-two), try putting "World Traveler". If we were interviewing you and saw this on your resume, it would prompt a series of powerful questions that you could respond to with excitement.

Fifty-Two
Loyalty, Perception vs. Reality, Humbleness

Loyalty - you better have it! If you don't have loyalty, you will not receive loyalty in return! Business is business. In today's fast, globalized economy, one thing is still key to holding customers for life: loyalty! If you show loyalty to your customers, they will show loyalty to you and your business. How do you know when loyalty of a customer to your business has been achieved? It is when that loyal customer uses word-of-mouth marketing in a positive manner with everyone he or she knows. Be loyal and stay loyal to your customers, and your customers will be loyal and stay loyal to you!

Perception vs. Reality: How do you think others perceive you? Do you think your customers would pay for what you are doing right now?

Humbleness: Be thankful for everything you have! Humbleness keeps you grounded and is one true key to being successful. One way to learn how to ensure you stay grounded, which will afford you greater dividends in the long run, is to continually evaluate if you are in fact grounded.

Ask yourself an obvious question about humbleness: "When was the last time I unwittingly found myself immersed in aiding someone else with no conscious gain intended for myself?" Or better yet, "Which external (Chapter Twenty) volunteer organizations, am I participating in at the present time?"

Wrap Up
Tuning in for Success...

Stand up, get out, and get on with your life! Do NOT tell yourself you can't, just go do it NOW!

This book is an essential guide for the mission on which you are now embarking. Read the entire thing and re-read it as many times as necessary, until the key points you feel are essential to your success start working for you. Not everything in this book will work for everyone. We know this. However, without tools, study guides, and educational literature, there is NO way you will be able to fully achieve your success and tap into the powerful *"Well Of Greatness©"* that lies within you!

We want you to be successful – that is why we wrote this book. Share the book's ideas with your coworkers, family members, and friends. Teach them the tools necessary for success. Every time you do this, it will further enhance your knowledge and application of the tools in this book.

This will also make you a successful and better person for helping others!

By starting close to home, *"What's In It For Me"* (WIIFM) you will be able to recognize how to tune into a much greater station ... *"WHAT'S IN IT FOR humankind"!*

...Go Do It Now!

WIIFM
Additional Momentum
Enhancement Options

1. To push your fast-track success quotient, explore an explosive e-Course on *"ADVANCING IN YOUR CAREER©"* by going to www.JeffreyMagee.com. Enter the e-Center for power success.

2. Ensure that you remain tuned in to WIIFM success ideas and techniques on a weekly basis by enrolling in the weekly syndicated **Leadership Moment©** column at www.JeffreyMagee.com. Go to the eZine Center for success!

3. Arbitrarily put a note on any date, for ten consecutive weeks, in your day planner or electronic planning device (PDA) to review the notes within this book, a recent workshop participant workbook you have completed, or class lecture material. By making these notes, when that day arrives and you reference your planning device, there will be a subtle note to reinforce the ideas which you have previously committed to adopting and adapting into your daily behavioral patterns for success!

4. Greater WIIFM opportunities can be experienced at: www.WIIFM.org and/or www.WIIFM.us

5. Daily Action Plans Map For Success. Take a small piece of paper or a 3x5 index card and write down the "What's in it for me factor" that are most crucial to your immediate success. Place them in areas where you will see them each morning when you wake, each midday, and each night before you go to bed. This will allow you to consciously see the desired WIIFM technique all day. By continually seeing the WIIFM goal, you increase your likelihood of attaining that objective.

6. If you e-mail either of the authors, they will send you a power list of ten additional WIIFM enhancement ideas to ensure even greater success. You can reach them at Jeffrey@JeffreyMagee.com and Damon@JeffreyMagee.com.

WIIFM
About The Authors

To Arrange A Speaking Appearance, Contact
Robert@JeffreyMagee.com or call
Toll free: 1-877-90-MAGEE

Jeff Magee, Ph.D., PDM, CSP, CMC is a highly sought after content-rich platform speaker, author and consultant who works with individuals and businesses that wish to greatly increase their productivity and profitability through business and leadership training without limits. His fourteen books have been transcribed into five foreign editions, and he has had three best sellers. He also serves as the publisher of *PERFORMANCE* magazine. His training firm and staff have increased net revenues every year for more than a decade. For more information and to see other exciting resource books, audio and video titles, go to www.JeffreyMagee.com/Library.asp.

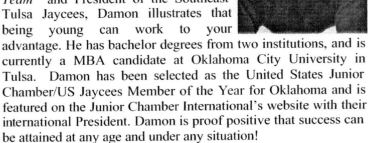

Damon Roberts is a high-energy leader, recognized as the top salesman in two different industries in which he has worked, and is a community activist. As a member of Tulsa Mayor Bill LaFortune's *"Performance Review Team"* and President of the Southeast Tulsa Jaycees, Damon illustrates that being young can work to your advantage. He has bachelor degrees from two institutions, and is currently a MBA candidate at Oklahoma City University in Tulsa. Damon has been selected as the United States Junior Chamber/US Jaycees Member of the Year for Oklahoma and is featured on the Junior Chamber International's website with their international President. Damon is proof positive that success can be attained at any age and under any situation!

WIIFM ("What's in it for me") **Gift, Wallet Reminder Card:**
This wallet reminder card can be folded and torn/cut out from this page and carried in your day planner, portfolio, laminated and left on your desk as a quick reference guide to "What's in it for me" engagement techniques...

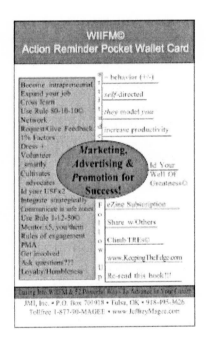